U.S. Department of Justice
Office of Justice Programs
National Institute of Justice

OCT. 09

NIJ

Research for  Practice

Learning From 9/11

*Organizational Change in the New York City
and Arlington County, Va., Police Departments*

www.ojp.usdoj.gov/nij

U.S. Department of Justice

Office of Justice Programs

810 Seventh Street N.W.

Washington, DC 20531

Eric H. Holder, Jr.
Attorney General

Laurie O. Robinson
Acting Assistant Attorney General

Kristina Rose
Acting Director, National Institute of Justice

This and other publications and products
of the National Institute of Justice can be
found at:

National Institute of Justice
www.ojp.usdoj.gov/nij

Office of Justice Programs
Innovation • Partnerships • Safer Neighborhoods
www.ojp.usdoj.gov

OCT. 09

Learning From 9/11: Organizational Change in the New York City and Arlington County, Va., Police Departments

Gwen Holden, Gerard Murphy, Corina Solé Brito and Joshua Ederheimer

This Research for Practice summarizes a more detailed study prepared by Gwen Holden, Gerard Murphy, Corina Solé Brito and Joshua Ederheimer of the Police Executive Research Forum.

The opinions and conclusions expressed in this document are solely those of the authors and do not necessarily reflect the views of the U.S. Department of Justice or the National Institute of Justice.

This research was supported by grant number 2002-IJ-CX-0013 from the National Institute of Justice to the Police Executive Research Forum.

NCJ 227346

ABOUT THIS REPORT

On Sept. 11, 2001, local first responders in two jurisdictions — New York City and Arlington County, Va. — were forced to deal with attacks on the World Trade Center and the Pentagon that were unprecedented in scope and loss of life. Following 9/11, the National Institute of Justice awarded a grant to the Police Executive Research Forum (PERF) to conduct case studies of the two law enforcement agencies most directly involved to learn what they could teach about best practices for responding to future incidents.

What did the researchers find?

- Proactive intelligence gathering within the community about terrorist threats and sharing that information within and among agencies are key to preventing and responding to terrorist attacks.

- Counterterrorism policing is the same as crime policing.

- The first priority in responding to a terrorist attack is to save lives, including those of first responders. Setting up a secure perimeter and avoiding over-responding to an initial attack can prevent loss of life in a second, more devastating attack.

- Both the New York City Police Department and the Arlington County Police Department have greatly expanded counterterrorism training at all levels and have integrated that training into traditional police training exercises.

- Setting up a media relations plan is essential to get accurate information out to both family members of victims and the general public, to control rumors and prevent the spread of misinformation, and to ensure that the presence of media does not interfere with evacuation and rescue efforts and traffic control.

Who should read this study?

Chiefs and managers of law enforcement and other first-responder agencies.

Gwen Holden, Gerard Murphy, Corina Solé Brito and Joshua Ederheimer

Learning From 9/11: Organizational Change in the New York City and Arlington County, Va., Police Departments

About the Authors

Gwen Holden,
Gerard Murphy,
Corina Solé Brito and
Joshua Ederheimer are
with the Police Executive
Research Forum.

The attacks on the World Trade Center and the Pentagon on Sept. 11, 2001, were among the most dramatic events ever to have occurred on U.S. soil. They were unprecedented attacks by terrorists against icons of American commercial and military power. Although federal and state agencies have become involved in handling such incidents, the main responsibility for dealing with them falls to *local* law enforcement. The third report of the Advisory Panel to Assess Domestic Response Capabilities for Terrorism, issued three months after the Sept. 11 incidents, makes this point clearly: "All terrorist incidents are local or at least will start that way. Effective response and recovery can only be achieved with the recognition that local responders are the first line of defense."[1]

Little exists in the way of "best practices" to help agencies prepare for and manage an incident of this importance. To help develop such best practices, the National Institute of Justice (NIJ) awarded a grant to the Police Executive Research Forum (PERF) to conduct case studies of the two law enforcement agencies most directly involved on Sept. 11 — the New York City Police Department (NYPD) and the Arlington County, Va., Police Department. PERF staff interviewed agency representatives and reviewed internal documents to create the recommendations presented here. This report summarizes a more detailed study prepared by PERF. The police departments involved may have made additional changes since the original fieldwork that is not reflected in this report. This project is not a side-by-side comparison of the two agencies. Making such a comparison would be a disservice to both. First, the agencies responded to two different incidents in terms of

loss of life and property damage. Second, the two agencies and the jurisdictions they serve, although similar in some regards, are different in many ways. Exhibit 1 shows some of the key differences between the jurisdictions.

New York City Police Department Case Study

Unlike most major American cities, New York City had experience with terrorist incidents long before the attacks of Sept. 11, 2001. On Feb. 26, 1993, a truck bomb exploded in the parking garage beneath the World Trade Center, leaving six dead and more than 1,000 injured. In June 1993, the FBI arrested eight people for plotting to bomb the Lincoln and Holland tunnels, major bridges, and the United Nations headquarters building.

On Sept. 11, 2001, the New York City Police Department had about 36,000 sworn officers and 14,000 civilian employees, making it the largest law enforcement agency in the world. A total of 2,749 people died in the World Trade Center attacks on Sept. 11, the largest loss of life from a hostile attack on U.S. soil in the nation's history. The New York City Fire Department suffered 343 fatalities — the largest loss of life of any emergency

Exhibit 1. New York City and Arlington County, Va., 2000

	Arlington County	New York City
Total population	189,453	8,008,278
Total housing units	90,246	3,200,912
Total sworn officers	483	36,000
Officers per 1,000 residents	2.5	4.5
Number of patrol areas	4 districts	76 precincts

Sources: "Population, Housing Units, Area, and Density: 2000," U.S. Census Bureau website, www.census.gov; Reaves, Brian A., and Hickman, Matthew J., *Law Enforcement Management and Administrative Statistics, 2000: Data for Individual State and Local Agencies with 100 or More Officers,* Washington, D.C.: U.S. Department of Justice, Office of Justice Programs, Bureau of Justice Statistics, March 2004, available online at www.ojp.usdoj.gov/bjs/pub/pdf/lemas00.pdf; Arlington, Va., Police Department website, Main Page, www.arlingtonva.us/Departments/Police/PoliceMain.aspx.

response agency in history. The Port Authority Police Department, a specialized law enforcement agency of 1,600 employees, suffered 37 fatalities — the largest loss of life of any police force in history. The NYPD suffered 23 fatalities — the second largest loss of life of any police force in history. All told, 72 law enforcement officers perished on Sept. 11, 2001.[2]

The ever-present specter of a future terrorist attack has provided the backdrop for, and given a sense of urgency to, shaping the NYPD's counterterrorism strategy. That has been no easy job, nor is combating terrorism likely to decrease in importance within the department in the future. "It has taken constant attention. It's extremely difficult," Police Commissioner Raymond W. Kelly says. "But make no mistake: It's something we have to do ourselves."[3]

Introducing a new mindset on counterterrorism readiness: Organizational changes within the NYPD

Within one month of taking office in January 2002, Commissioner Kelly revamped the NYPD's Intelligence Division (ID) and created a new counterterrorism presence within the department.

The Counter Terrorism Bureau. The NYPD's Counter Terrorism Bureau (CTB) is managed by the Deputy Commissioner of Counter Terrorism. The CTB, with 205 officers, works with the FBI's Joint Terrorism Task Forces. The CTB analyzes the worldwide terrorist threat for NYPD executives, runs counterterrorism training exercises for NYPD personnel, does research, and develops plans for protecting key sites within New York City.

The Intelligence Division. According to one Intelligence Division official, the division today is "very different than what it was before" 9/11. Before 9/11, primary responsibilities of the division were protecting dignitaries and developing criminal intelligence. Today, one division official stated, the ID is "proactively" engaged in efforts to detect and prevent terrorism. Division personnel are devoting 95 percent of their work to examining possible links to terrorism before an event occurs.

Developing intelligence and investigative leads. With the FBI's Joint Terrorism Task

"It has taken constant attention. It's extremely difficult," Police Commissioner Raymond W. Kelly says. "But make no mistake: It's something we have to do ourselves."

Rumor control is better served by sharing facts as they become available rather than allowing incorrect and misleading reports to fill an information vacuum.

Forces, personnel from the NYPD's Intelligence Division and Counter Terrorism Bureau and the department's counterterrorism hotline are key parts of intelligence gathering. Field intelligence officers are assigned to the NYPD's 76 precincts as well as commands at the borough, housing, transit and school levels.[4] Through Operation Nexus, the NYPD actively encourages businesses to notice anything unusual or suspicious and to report such instances to authorities.[5]

Controlling rumors and misinformation. The department has also revamped how it communicates with the news media and the public. Officials of the NYPD's Public Information Division say that their experience on 9/11 underscored the importance of getting the facts to the media as they emerge during a critical incident. Rumor control is better served by sharing facts as they become available rather than allowing incorrect and misleading reports to fill an information vacuum.

The Public Information Division's media contact list reflects efforts to reach large and small media outlets the public is most likely to turn to for information in an emergency. The division has

expanded its contact list to 200 media outlets.

Since 9/11, the Public Information Division also has been holding training exercises to perfect its ability to set up a media staging area during a critical incident. One division official explained that media staging is critical during an emergency because reporters at a critical incident site can interfere with first responders' evacuation and rescue efforts and traffic control.

Training officers in counterterrorism tactics

The work of the NYPD's Training Bureau today reflects a philosophy of training all NYPD officials in anti-terrorism tactics and procedures. Prevention, say Training Bureau officials, is all about broadening officers' perspective on terrorism and encouraging them to "think abstractly and globally" about counterterrorism measures. Achieving these objectives, these officials continued, begins with increasing officers' awareness of the threat of terrorism. The NYPD's recruit training curriculum includes a new section on terrorism prevention.

Response-related training focuses on saving lives, including those of first responders. According to a Training Bureau official, NYPD officers are now taught that setting up a strong, secure and safe inner perimeter is the first order of business at the site of a critical incident. Officers also are taught that an incident may be only the first in what terrorists have planned as a series of attacks. Thus, first responders are cautioned not to rush into the target site, where they could be injured or killed in a later attack. Nor should they "over respond" to an early incident that may be intended by terrorists to divert responders' attention away from a second, more devastating attack.

Counterterrorism operations in the field and on patrol

The Special Operations Division. The Special Operations Division (SOD) is an important part of the NYPD's efforts to prevent a future terrorist attack. A unit of the NYPD's Patrol Services Bureau, the SOD has more than 400 sworn and civilian personnel. Its primary role is to protect potential terrorist targets in the city. That role,

one division official explained, is carried out in close collaboration with the Intelligence Division. Everything the SOD does, this official continued, is "funneled through" the ID. "We get a list of hard and soft targets" from the ID, this official noted, and the department uses directed patrols to protect these sites under Operation Hercules, which has been operational since before Sept. 11, 2001. Strategically, the Hercules teams' objective is to disrupt terrorists' surveillance of New York City landmarks or other potential targets by "providing the appearance of a randomized, heavily armed police presence," one official explained. At each site, "we 'show the flag,' deploy, and look for anything suspicious."

The SOD works closely with the U.S. Coast Guard in observing and surveying potential targets such as bridges, tunnels, air vents that open onto water sites, and marinas. The SOD worked with the city's Department of Health to train SOD personnel in the use of air-monitoring "meters" to detect possible radioactive material. The Department of Health runs the city's Biowatch. It alerts the SOD about calls reporting the presence of a suspected biological substance, such as

Response-related training focuses on saving lives, including those of first responders.

a white powder suspected to be anthrax.

The Operations Division. The NYPD's Operations Division (OD) is the communications link between the executive command and the police officer on the street. The OD coordinates all personnel details for the department, including those placed with special events and emergency incidents. According to one OD official, the division "acts as the information hub of the NYPD" during an emergency, running the NYPD's Emergency Operations Center (EOC), which, in turn, communicates information to command staff and watch commanders. According to an OD official, the division's telephone communications system includes digital, cellular, satellite and analog capabilities. The EOC also manages and promotes interagency cooperation during a critical incident. The EOC's responsibilities during a critical incident include:

- Providing 24-hour-a-day monitoring of any major incident in the city, from building collapses to major crimes.

- Tracking all officer-related information arising from or occurring during an

incident, including line-of-duty injuries, resignations and suspensions as well as misconduct by any city employee.

- Coordinating all personnel placement planning for scheduled events.

- Coordinating all requests for more police personnel during scheduled and unscheduled events, assessing whether requests are necessary and reasonable, and making the final determination of how many officers to place in response to a request.

- Coordinating moving on-duty personnel assigned to the eight borough task forces.

The Disorder Control Unit. The department created the Disorder Control Unit (DCU) in 1992 in the aftermath of three days of rioting in the Crown Heights neighborhood of Brooklyn in August 1991. The unit is charged with "the mission of preventing and suppressing civil disorder" within New York City, whether planned or spontaneous. The DCU works closely with the patrol boroughs, including conducting drills, tabletop and no-notice exercises to ensure readiness. It identifies

sites within NYPD precincts that could be targets for civil disorder or a terrorist attack, and develops response plans.

The Community Affairs Unit. The NYPD's Community Affairs Unit is charged with reassuring the public in an emergency and setting up a mass casualty and missing persons center at the incident site. For unit officials, 9/11 was a learning experience. They had to set up and manage a mass casualty center quickly. There had been no planning for such a center before the Sept. 11 attack, one unit official explained.

The Performance Analysis Section. Since 9/11, the Performance Analysis Section of the NYPD Personnel Bureau's Employee Management Division has assigned a priority to improving its ability to reach out to and provide psychological counseling services for NYPD personnel during emergencies. A critical part of this mission has centered on overcoming long-standing fears among police agency personnel that admitting to and seeking help for emotional or psychological problems will have negative effects for their careers.

Major conclusions and lessons

Defining the organizational philosophy

Incorporate a counterterrorism philosophy throughout the department. Police Commissioner Raymond W. Kelly described the department's post-9/11 philosophy as "thinking about the unthinkable — what a few years ago was the unthinkable."[6]

Create a counterterrorism role within the department. Commissioner Kelly revamped the NYPD's Intelligence Division and created the new Counter Terrorism Bureau.

Recognize that counterterrorism policing is the same as crime policing. The department's emphasis on counterterrorism is premised on the belief that terrorism policing is the same as crime policing. Moreover, because terrorist groups commit traditional crimes to finance their work, good police work will uncover terrorist groups and their plans.

Police Commissioner Raymond W. Kelly described the department's post-9/11 philosophy as "thinking about the unthinkable — what a few years ago was the unthinkable."

Appoint specific people to drive the counterterrorism philosophy. Commissioner Kelly created the position of counterterrorism inspector, assigning an inspector to each NYPD patrol borough and major command. The inspectors work for the deputy commissioner for counterterrorism and serve as the point people on terrorism issues for the borough chiefs and precinct commanders.[7]

Educate the community. Consistent with its internal changes, the department has set up a public awareness campaign to increase the community's understanding about terrorism, including its role in noting potential terrorist activity and reporting it to the police.

Building organizational capabilities

Provide up-to-date counterterrorism information to officers. The Counter Terrorism Bureau prepares daily terrorism "briefing packages" that are tailored to various audiences within the department.

Get intelligence information to the patrol officer and provide the patrol officer with access to the intelligence information collector.

Patrol officers are in the best position to identify suspicious events within their assigned areas.

Train new officers in counterterrorism tactics. Counterterrorism training begins at the recruit level. An innovative part of that training includes providing recruits with a daily one- to two-page summary that highlights reports of terrorism-related activity around the world.

Train the patrol force. A new roll-call training program is introduced every month. Instructors spend 20 minutes per roll-call training session discussing such topics as counterintelligence and information gathering.

Conduct counterterrorism training in large groups. NYPD training for all personnel occurs in large groups and includes first responders from other city emergency response agencies and neighboring law enforcement agencies.

Train police managers to lead and make good decisions. NYPD police executives receive training in standing up a command post and mobilizing to mount an incident response.

Preventing terrorist incidents

Regularly assess the vulnerability of your community's assets. The Counter Terrorism Bureau conducts extensive assessments of vulnerable sites within the city.

Keep a proactive intelligence role. Gathering intelligence involves fostering a sense of confidence in the department so the public is willing to provide information, and developing good confidential informants.

Engage in strategic terrorist threat assessment. Keep a detailed awareness of groups or individuals worldwide who may be interested in targeting the United States or your community.

Reach out to local and regional businesses (including businesses outside your agency's jurisdiction) as intelligence sources. The NYPD's Nexus Program was created as a bridge between the department and businesses within a 150-mile radius of the city that potentially could be exploited by groups or individuals in support of terrorist activities.

Randomized presence can be an effective deterrent. The department's high-visibility Hercules Teams are used to interrupt surveillance of potential targets by any terrorist cells working in the city.

Collaborate with organizations to leverage expertise. The Special Operations Division works closely with the U.S. Coast Guard in observing and surveying potential targets such as bridges, tunnels, marinas, and air vents that open onto water sites. The SOD has also developed a partnership with the city's Department of Health to train SOD personnel in the use of air-monitoring "meters" to detect possible radioactive material and to respond to calls reporting the presence of other potential radiological and biological threats, such as white powders that could be anthrax.

Preparing for a critical incident

Before an incident, appoint a lead agency to avoid conflict. Since 9/11, the city has rewritten its emergency operations plan, which identifies the authorities and responsibilities of emergency services agencies during critical incidents.

Plan responses based on geographical areas and responsibility. The NYPD keeps and annually updates disorder control plans that contain information about critical and sensitive locations within each precinct.

Prepare for outside agencies to respond and help. The NYPD has mutual aid agreements with law enforcement agencies to provide help during critical incidents.

Ensure that all personnel know their responsibilities. Specialized response units know their responsibilities and train for them regularly.

Plan for the response of off-duty officers. Procedures for recalling off-duty officers are critical during an emergency.

Control rumors and misinformation. Public Information Division officials say that quelling the spread of rumors is a priority during a critical incident.

Meet the needs of the public and victims. Police agencies, with other emergency response agencies, must develop plans for setting up mass casualty centers. These centers are the primary point of contact for individuals who are desperately seeking information about the whereabouts and condition of family members or friends. "Line management" is a critical part of establishing order. Crowds can become volatile, and keeping people as comfortable as possible and informed of the process is essential. Food and water must be available to people waiting in line.

Improve mental health outreach and services. Employee assistance resources must be visible and readily accessible to agency personnel.

Arlington County Police Department Case Study

Arlington County, Va., is an urban county of slightly less than 26 square miles, making it the smallest county in area in the United States. Located directly across the Potomac River from Washington, D.C., the county has no incorporated cities or towns. The county had a residential population of 189,453 in 2000, according to the Census Bureau. The daytime population is much larger on workdays; the county has more than 196,000 jobs. The Pentagon alone has a workforce of more than 23,000 military and civilian personnel. In addition, about 25,000 people visit Arlington's tourist attractions each day, including the Arlington National Cemetery, the Iwo Jima Memorial, and the Pentagon. Ronald Reagan National Airport has an average of 50,000 passengers daily.[8]

The Arlington County Police Department (ACPD) provides law enforcement services to Arlington County's residential and business communities. On the day of the attack, the department had an approved strength of 362 full-time sworn officers and 85 civilian staff. However, the department's sworn strength was closer to 320. Moreover, on Sept. 11, 2001, a significant number of the command staff were out of town at various conferences and a staff retreat. The ACPD provides 24-hour protection, using three shifts to patrol 10 police beats within four districts that follow the natural boundaries within Arlington County.

The Arlington County Fire Department, the ACPD, and the Pentagon's Defense Protective Service all act under an Incident Command System (ICS) in responding to emergencies. However, on Sept. 11 terrorists attacked the Pentagon, which is no ordinary building. An enormous complex, the Pentagon houses critical national security offices. Although the Pentagon is in Arlington County, it is a U.S. military facility under the direct control of the Secretary of Defense. The Defense Protective Service controls access to the building.

Assessing emergency preparedness in the aftermath of 9/11

On July 23, 2002, Arlington County officials released a report that examined the county's response to the 9/11 attack.[9] The report, funded by the U.S. Department of Justice, Office of Justice Programs, assessed practices employed during the 9/11 response. The report highlighted strengths of the county's 9/11 response. These included management of mutual aid assets and outside support, adherence to the county's Comprehensive Emergency Management Plan, and use of the county's employee assistance program.[10]

. . . in the aftermath of the 9/11 attack, teaching the incident command philosophy at the command and line officer levels alike has become a priority.

Improving police preparedness

Targets for possible terrorist attacks. Arlington County is a "target-rich" environment, ACPD officials noted, that has numerous government agencies and installations that might be potential targets for a terrorist attack. ACPD officials list 120 targets based on threat assessments carried out by ACPD district commanders. These targets include the Pentagon; Reagan National Airport; bridges into Washington, D.C.; Washington Metropolitan Area Transit Authority subway stations; and the offices of the U.S. Drug Enforcement Administration, the Federal Deposit Insurance Corporation and the U.S. Marshals Service.

Advancing the ICS and emergency management planning. ACPD officials reported that in the aftermath of the 9/11 attack, teaching the incident command philosophy at the command and line officer levels alike has become a priority. The need to bring training in ICS "down to the officer level" is reinforced by a central principle of the ICS approach — that "anyone who responds may have to take charge of an incident," one

official noted. In addition, the ACPD is aware of the addition of ICS standards that police agencies must meet for accreditation purposes (e.g., by the Commission on Accreditation for Law Enforcement Agencies). To help with this mission, the *After-Action Report* recommended that all command officers and supervisors receive a pocket-sized field guide containing instructions for setting up law enforcement ICS roles.[11] The assistant chief who sketched out the ACPD's first incident response plan on 9/11 agrees. She said she based her actions on 9/11 on a card that she carries that spells out the central steps in developing an ICS. She received that card in an incident command course sponsored by the International Association of Chiefs of Police in the early 1990s.

Training in support of ICS. ACPD officials reported that training for critical incidents, "both mass and smaller attacks," has increased significantly since 9/11. According to these officials, ACPD training now covers active-shooter incidents, hazardous materials, and "general education on domestic and international terrorism."

The training curriculum for ACPD recruits now includes

terrorism topics. The number and frequency of tabletop exercises in ICS also have increased, officials say. A recent exercise involved local, state and federal law enforcement agencies; the fire service; the public health agency; airport security; and the Virginia Hospital Center, a major medical facility in Arlington County.

ACPD officials used the opportunity provided by a mock exercise at the Pentagon to test hospital and police cooperation as they work out a security plan with area hospitals. The ACPD chief has told officers to respond directly to the hospital "if they hear anything on the radio" signaling that an incident has occurred that may require a hospital lockdown. "Hospitals are strategic assets," one ACPD official asserted. A hospital lockdown requires law enforcement officials' help to secure the buildings, control traffic and set up decontamination lines for an incident involving a biological or chemical agent.

Upgrading communications abilities. ACPD uses the U.S. Government Emergency Telecommunications Service, a Department of Homeland Security program designed to ensure that key people can use the telephone system even if it becomes overloaded. Several ACPD officials have priority access to cell phones by punching in certain codes. Since 9/11, critical entities such as the Virginia Hospital Center, the county health department and the county public school system have bought police radios to ensure seamless communication in an attack or other critical incident.

Confronting the results of hypervigilance. ACPD officials reported that the heightened state of alert that has been in effect constantly since 9/11 is creating stress and frustration among ACPD personnel. In particular, one department official noted, officials of the county's Office of Emergency Management (OEM) "always are on top of our cops" to remain hypervigilant. ACPD officials' comments also suggest that OEM officials' hypervigilance post-9/11 is not the only source of pressure that department personnel feel. Keeping emergency services personnel countywide in a high-alert status tries their patience. "Since 9/11, we've had the anthrax scare,

a winter storm, the sniper case, and a hurricane," an official said.

Coordinating intelligence sharing countywide

One ACPD official said initiatives to prevent terrorist attacks should begin "way back in the intel stage." Since 9/11, the ACPD, in fact, has improved intelligence coordination countywide. ACPD officials reported that briefings are held regularly with representatives of the Pentagon, the Department of Homeland Security, and the Metropolitan Washington Council of Governments (Metro COG). The Metro COG meetings have facilitated regional information sharing. The ACPD also takes part in weekly regional conference calls hosted by the FBI. Other participants include area police chiefs; the Bureau of Alcohol, Tobacco, Firearms and Explosives; and representatives of the military.[12]

In addition, one official explained, the ACPD "could do a better job with data-sharing" within the department to reduce conflict around the issue of defining the "need to know" during sensitive operations. During the October 2002 sniper case that resulted in the deaths of 10 individuals in the Washington, D.C., Maryland, and northern and central Virginia regions, some department officials felt that other officials were inappropriately keeping information from them.[13]

Improving collaboration with other responders

ACPD officials said ties with federal agencies since the 9/11 attack have been "good for some time," but there is a need to address internal issues that inhibit the transfer of information between federal and local agencies. Experiences with the FBI, in particular, have been extensive and favorable.

According to ACPD officials, since 9/11 a mutual aid agreement has been completed with the Pentagon. Importantly, the updated agreement allows the ACPD to have concurrent jurisdiction on Pentagon grounds (i.e., outside the building) for criminal and traffic concerns, if necessary.

The ACPD has appointed liaisons to preserve regular contact with the Arlington

County Fire Department and the Pentagon. In addition, protocols for engaging mutual aid partners in future emergencies require that responding agencies contact the requesting agency before sending help.

Strengthening community ties

Communications between the ACPD and the public have improved since 9/11. ACPD officials believe the Arlington County community "feels the hypervigilance" that its emergency services personnel are experiencing post-9/11, but expects that police and fire officials can handle it. Volunteers have helped develop "Arlington Alert," an emergency e-mail and text messaging service. Citizens can sign up to receive the service.[14]

The county has bought a radio station and is testing a siren system, both for alerting residents. Community emergency response teams (CERT teams) have been set up within the county to enlist citizen volunteers in performing "some light emergency response duties" if first responders cannot immediately get to a site. CERT teams currently include some 120 to 140 volunteers. Team members are not certified, but receive training in search and rescue, firefighting, first aid, freeing victims from buildings and vehicles, and traffic control. An ACPD official said that experience with CERT team volunteers during Hurricane Isabel served as a model for integrating them into future incidents.

Major conclusions and recommendations

Preventing terrorist incidents

Expand intelligence-sharing efforts. Realizing that initiatives to prevent terrorist attacks should begin as early as possible, the ACPD has improved intelligence coordination countywide.

Conduct threat assessments of local assets. The ACPD now has access to a list of 120 targets.

Engage residents in prevention activities. Community policing can provide avenues to engage residents in watching their neighborhoods for suspicious activities.

Command officers and supervisors should have pocket-sized field guides.

Preparing for a critical incident

Ensure the agency is adept at incident management. Training agency personnel to use the Incident Command System during a critical incident requires continual work to inculcate this idea into the department's culture.

Diligently prepare for outside law enforcement agencies to respond and help. Even in northern Virginia, where agencies regularly work together under mutual aid agreements, differences in the procedures and laws that govern the nature and extent of help can be exposed during the pressures that critical incidents impose on organizations.

Neighboring jurisdictions must coordinate assigning their personnel with the host agency. On Sept. 11, ACPD officials seemingly were overwhelmed at the staging area when mutual aid officers arrived without notice that they were on their way.

Coordinate traffic management and evacuation protocols. One jurisdiction's decision to evacuate can have an enormous influence on traffic in neighboring jurisdictions.

Develop strong ties with other emergency responders in the jurisdiction. Police, fire, emergency medical and emergency management agencies all play key roles during a critical incident.

Develop protocols with emergency medical services and hospitals. Develop a plan with local emergency medical services and local hospitals for transporting the injured to area hospitals, including provisions for hospital diversions because of closures or inadequate capacity at some facilities and excess capacity at others.

Exercise plans regularly. Developing plans is not enough. They have to be exercised, reviewed and adjusted.

Include private security. Include private-sector property managers and private security in training and exercises.

Ensure that every officer is prepared. ACPD personnel now have specific procedures and protocols to follow when alerted to the threat of a terrorist attack.

Provide agency managers with policies and procedures. Command officers and supervisors should have pocket-sized field guides.

Keep enough local and regional maps in command vehicles. The ACPD has placed maps of the area in command supervisory vehicles.

Provide officers with equipment and ensure that it works. Since 9/11, the ACPD has bought better equipment for department personnel, including personally fitted masks.

Organize and use citizen volunteers. Community emergency response teams have been set up within the county to enlist citizen volunteers in performing light emergency response duties if first responders cannot immediately get to a site.

Develop and exercise protocols for on-scene management. Improve protocols for coordinating response units and the incident command post.

Review procedures for setting up perimeters. If an outer perimeter is set up too close to the incident site, a significant portion of the on-site incident command may be placed at risk if there is another attack.

On-scene personnel need to be identified and controlled. The influx of people at the scene may require developing an identification system for use in controlling access to incident sites.

Develop a system for telling officers about assignments and shift changes. Supervisors and line officers need timely notice of assignments and regular status updates during a critical incident.

Check officers to prevent fatigue. Ensure that officers do not work more than one 12-hour shift without rest unless necessary.

Be prepared to address both immediate and long-term effects of the incident on first responders and their family members. Call on local mental health or employee programs and outside groups such as the Red Cross, which has specific units trained in addressing first responders' mental health concerns in response to disasters.

Communicate with residents. Agencies need to work with government leaders to develop and institutionalize procedures for warning citizens of a terrorist attack and keeping the public informed about post-attack conditions.

The principles for preventing and responding to traditional crimes and terrorism are the same.

Be prepared to receive donations and volunteers. Donated goods and volunteers can overwhelm an agency.

Set up a media relations plan. This plan should include where to stage the media and who will deliver briefings.

Observations and Implications for Law Enforcement From New York City and Arlington County's Experiences

Coordination is fundamental to a successful response to any critical incident (e.g., weather-related disasters, terrorist attacks, significant fires, major crime scenes). Although the federal government has produced response guidelines,[15] many state and local emergency response agencies have improved coordination themselves.

The private sector is on the front line of homeland security efforts and is important to identifying and finding terrorists as well as disrupting terrorist networks. According to the Department of Homeland Security, the private sector oversees about 85 percent of the nation's critical infrastructure.[16] The experiences of the New York City Police Department and the Arlington County Police Department can provide perspectives that will help law enforcement agencies develop effective strategies and approaches to make our communities safer. Though very different in size and organizational structure, these two agencies provide many similar lessons learned.

Defining an organizational strategy

- Incorporate a counterterrorism philosophy throughout the department.

- Create a counterterrorism role within the department.

- Embrace the notion that anti-terrorism policing is the same as crime policing. The principles for preventing and responding to traditional crimes and terrorism are the same.

- Choose specific personnel to drive the counterterrorism philosophy.

- Educate the public about its role and the department's initiatives.

- Recognize that community policing principles can help law enforcement meet

the demands of homeland security.

Building organizational abilities

- Provide up-to-date counterterrorism information to officers.

- Get intelligence information to the street officer and provide the street officer with access to the intelligence information collector.

- Train officers in counterterrorism tactics.

- Conduct counterterrorism training in large groups.

- Train police managers in critical incident management.

Preventing terrorist incidents

- Regularly assess your community's vulnerable or valuable assets that might be targeted by terrorists.

- Keep a proactive intelligence role.

- Reach out to local and regional businesses as intelligence sources.

- Use randomized presence as a deterrent.

- Collaborate with emergency response organizations to leverage expertise.

- Build regional intelligence talent.

- Engage residents in prevention activities.

- Develop information-sharing protocols with other agencies. The FBI, the Department of Homeland Security and local law enforcement should share intelligence information with other emergency service providers, such as fire and emergency management officials.

Preparing for a critical incident

- Cities and counties should conduct vulnerability assessments and gather information about potential targets, and then share those results with neighboring jurisdictions to develop a regional understanding of risks and threats.

- Learn from the best practices established by other agencies.

Institute counterterrorism training at all levels of local law enforcement — from line officers to command level to the chief executive level.

■ Develop strong relationships with other emergency responders — fire, emergency medical and emergency services — in your jurisdiction.

■ Before an incident, choose a lead agency to avoid conflict.

■ Plan responses based on geographical areas and responsibilities.

■ Develop protocols with emergency medical services and hospitals.

■ Ensure that the agency is adept at incident management. Local law enforcement and other emergency responders must incorporate the National Incident Management System[17] into emergency response plans.

■ Prepare for outside agencies to respond and help, including coordinating assigning their personnel with the host agency.

■ Coordinate traffic management and evacuation protocols with neighboring law enforcement agencies.

■ Exercise plans regularly. Conduct honest self-assessments after exercises and revise policy based on lessons learned.

■ Include private-sector property managers and private security in training and exercises. The partnerships could include target hardening through environmental design, other guidance, and response procedures for effective preparedness, prevention and response roles.

■ Institute counterterrorism training at all levels of local law enforcement — from line officers to command level to the chief executive level. Training should address street-level indicators of terrorism, the link between traditional crime and terrorism, information analysis, targeting and profiling issues, privacy concerns and other important ideas.

■ Focus training on area-specific target hazards. Train members from various disciplines simultaneously.

■ Embed counterterrorism training in existing training. Many agencies have developed creative methods to conduct training exercises that can serve as an example for others.

- Provide officers with equipment and ensure that it works.

- Plan for the response of your agency's off-duty officers.

- Provide agency managers with policies and procedures.

- Keep an acceptable supply of local and regional maps in command cars.

- Organize and use citizen volunteers.

- Plan for rumor control and misinformation.

- Improve mental health outreach and services for employees.

Responding to a critical incident

- Review procedures and criteria for setting up perimeters. Work together to set up zones and staging areas. Consider the possibility of second strikes. Where there is a potential biological, radiological or chemical hazard, there is also a need to stem contamination. First responders must work together to set up an exclusion or "hot" zone, a decontamination or "warm" zone, and a staging and support area or "cold" zone. The staging area should always be located upwind from the incident, preserved by trained personnel and protected by a secure crowd-control line.

- Create a method for easy identification and control of on-scene personnel.

- Develop a system for telling officers about developments and assignments.

- Check officers to prevent excessive fatigue.

- Be prepared to address both immediate and long-term effects of the incident on first responders and their family members.

- Communicate with residents about the incident and agency responses.

- Be prepared to receive donations and volunteers.

- Set up a media relations plan.

Notes

1. Advisory Panel to Assess Domestic Response Capabilities for Terrorism Involving Weapons of Mass Destruction (Gilmore Commission), *Third Annual Report to the*

President and the Congress of the Advisory Panel to Assess Domestic Response Capabilities for Terrorism Involving Weapons of Mass Destruction, December 15, 2001, p. 7. Available online at www.rand. org/nsrd/terrpanel.

2. This NYPD case study relies on the following sources: DeBlasio, Paul, Terrance Regan, Margaret Zinker, F. Brian Day, Michelle Crowder, Kathleen Bagdons, Robert Brodesky, and Dan Morin, "Effects of Catastrophic Events on Transportation System Management and Operations: New York City — September 11, 2001," draft report submitted to the U.S. Department of Transportation, ITS Joint Program Office, 2002; McKinsey & Co., *Improving NYPD Emergency Preparedness and Response,* New York: McKinsey & Co., 2002; McKinsey & Co., *Increasing FDNY's Preparedness,* New York: McKinsey & Co., 2002; National Commission on Terrorist Attacks Upon the United States, *The 9/11 Commission Report,* New York: W.W. Norton & Co., 2004 (hereinafter *9/11 Commission Report*); Thompson, Paul, and the Center for Cooperative Research, *The Terror Timeline,* New York: Regan Books, 2004.

3. Horowitz, Craig, "The NYPD's War on Terror," *New York Magazine,* Feb. 3, 2003. Available online at www.newyorkmetro.com/nymetro/news/features/n_8286/.

4. Although New York City is divided into five administrative units — the boroughs of Manhattan, Brooklyn, the Bronx, Queens and Staten Island — the NYPD subdivides Manhattan, Brooklyn and Queens into north and south, creating a total of eight patrol boroughs.

5. For more information about Operation Nexus, see the NYPD's Crime Prevention web page, www. nyc.gov/html/nypd/html/crime_prevention/counterterrorism.shtml.

6. Rashbaum, William K. and Judith Miller, "New York Police Training for Catastrophic Terrorism," *New York Times,* N.Y. Region, Feb. 15, 2004. Available online at www.nytimes. com/2004/02/15/nyregion/15THRE. html.

7. In the NYPD, the rank of inspector is the military equivalent of colonel.

8. This ACPD case study relies on the following sources: Carter, Mark R., Mark P. Howard, Nicholas Owens, David Register, Jason Kennedy, Kelley Pecheux, and Aaron Newton, "Effects of Catastrophic Events on Transportation System Management and Operations: The Pentagon and the National Capital Region — September 11, 2001," draft report submitted to the U.S. Department of Transportation, ITS Joint Program Office, Vienna, Va.: Science Applications International Corporation, 2002; National Commission on Terrorist Attacks Upon the United States, *9/11 Commission Report* (see note 2); Thompson and the Center for Cooperative Research, *The Terror Timeline* (see note 2); Titan Systems Corporation, *Arlington County: After-Action Report on the Response to the September 11 Terrorist Attack on the Pentagon,* Arlington, Va.: Titan Systems Corporation, 2002 (hereinafter *Arlington County After-Action Report*).

9. "Arlington County Creating Emergency Preparedness Blueprint from 9/11 After-Action Report Recommendations and First-hand Experience," Press Release, Arlington

County Public Affairs Division (July 23, 2002), available online at www.arlingtonva.us/NewsReleases/Scripts/ViewDetail.asp?Index=843.

10. Ibid.

11. Titan Systems Corporation, *Arlington County After-Action Report* (see note 8), p. C-19.

12. These weekly calls started after 9/11. In October 2002, during the Beltway Sniper experience, the calls became a daily occurrence.

13. For a complete report on law enforcement actions related to the Beltway Sniper case, see Murphy, Gerard R., and Chuck Wexler, *Managing a Multijurisdictional Case: Identifying the Lessons Learned From the Sniper Investigation,* Washington, D.C.: Police Executive Research Forum, 2004.

14. For more information on this service see the following website: www.arlingtonalert.com/index.php?CCheck=1.

15. For example, under Homeland Security Presidential Directive-5 (HSPD-5), the National Incident Management System (NIMS) "provides a consistent framework for incident management at all jurisdictional levels regardless of the cause, size or complexity of the incident." The National Response Framework uses NIMS and "establishes a comprehensive, national, all-hazards approach to domestic incident response." For more information, see U.S. Department of Homeland Security, *National Response Framework (NRF) — Fact Sheet,* n.d., available online at www.fema.gov/emergency/nrf/aboutNRF.htm.

16. See U.S. Department of Homeland Security, "Critical Infrastructure Sector Partnership" web page. Available online at www.dhs.gov/xprevprot/partnerships/editorial_0206.shtm.

17. See note 15 above.

Additional references

Jones, Radford W., Margaret A. Kowalk, and Patricia P. Miller. "Critical Incident Protocol — A Public and Private Partnership." East Lansing, Mich.: Michigan State University, School of Criminal Justice, 2000.

National Commission on Terrorist Attacks Upon the United States. Staff Statement No. 13: "Emergency Preparedness and Response" (n.d.). Available online at www.9-11commission.gov/staff_statements/staff_statement_13.pdf.

Safe Cities Project. Timothy P. Connors and Georgia Pellegrini, eds. *Hard Won Lessons: Policing Terrorism in the United States.* New York: The Center for Policing Terrorism at the Manhattan Institute, and Newark, N.J.: The Police Institute at Rutgers University, July 2005. Available online at www.manhattan-institute.org/pdf/scr_03.pdf.

Tierney, Kathleen J. "Strength of a City: A Disaster Research Perspective on the World Trade Center Attack," Social Science Research Council: Essays, July 18, 2002. Available online at www.ssrc.org/sept11/essays/tierney.htm.

The National Institute of Justice is the research, development, and evaluation agency of the U.S. Department of Justice. NIJ's mission is to advance scientific research, development, and evaluation to enhance the administration of justice and public safety.

The National Institute of Justice is a component of the Office of Justice Programs, which also includes the Bureau of Justice Assistance; the Bureau of Justice Statistics; the Community Capacity Development Office; the Office for Victims of Crime; the Office of Juvenile Justice and Delinquency Prevention; and the Office of Sex Offender Sentencing, Monitoring, Apprehending, Registering, and Tracking (SMART).

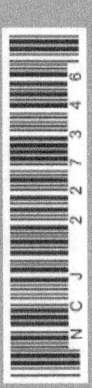

OCT. 09